Hip. Hip. Hallelujah!
DR. JOHN DEE JEFFRIES
EDITED BY C. GENEVIEVE JEFFRIES

Author of The Last Martyr; and, When I Can't Find God

VOLUME 3

PUBLISHED *by* PARABLES
Earthly Stories with a Heavenly Meaning

Hip. Hip. Hallelujah!
Volume 3:
Copyright © John Dee Jeffries
Author of The Last Martyr; When I Can't Find God and,
Hip. Hip. Hallelujah! Volumes 1, 2, & 3

Published By Parables

All Rights Reserved. No part of this book may be reproduced or utilized in any form or by any means, electronic or mechanical, including photocopying, recording, or by any information storage and retrieval system, without permission in writing from the author.

Unless otherwise specified Scripture quotations are taken from the authorized version of the King James Bible.

First Edition   June, 2017

ISBN 978-1-945698-15-6

Printed in the United States of America

Readers should be aware that Internet Web sites offered as citations and/or sources for further information may have been changed or disappeared between the time this was written and when it is read.

Illustration provided by www.unsplash.com

HIP. HIP. HALLELUJAH!
DR. JOHN DEE JEFFRIES
EDITED BY C. GENEVIEVE JEFFRIES
Author of The Last Martyr; and, When I Can't Find God
VOLUME 3

Knowing God
"You Guys Know God! I Don't"

A young fireman was electrocuted – a training accident – right in front of the firehouse!

His teeth shattered! The ends of his toes were blow off! Several of us held a spoon in his mouth to keep him from swallowing his tongue while others tried to hold him down as his body twitched and bounced on the hard concrete drive.

Afterward, the man who was responsible for the accidental electrocution, another fireman, came to talk to me and my friend Joe. Joe was my first convert – and a very strong Christian.

"You Guys Know God! I Don't. Would you guys pray, please pray, that God will keep him alive? John, Joe, I'm scared to death. Please ask God for me. You Guys Know God! I Don't."

These were strange words, strange words from a man who had constantly teased and taunted Joe and me because of our Christian faith. But, then again, perhaps these words were not so strange after all. You see, when the chips are down, I mean, when they're really down and you have no where to turn – people instinctively seek out God.

We did pray, Joe and I – and the young man miraculously survived….and, the taunting and teasing stopped.

There are many implications that could be drawn from this incident. I'll only focus on one: when your faith in Christ is visible, others may tease and taunt you; but, deep down, they know you have the real deal. The genuineness of your faith and its visibility, well, when the chips or down the fearful, the hurting, and yes, even the lost will draw strength and encouragement from you – and be nudged toward faith in Christ.

However, if you hide your light under a bushel. Or, If your testimony is tarnished, or If your character is questionable – or, If you conduct is suspect – or, If your conversation is crude and vulgar – why would anyone come to you or want what you have.

"You Guys Know God!" said he, "I Don't"

------ 000 ------

We began volumes one of the Hip. Hip. Hallelujah Collection by refering to what many today call "God-Things." These are the things that God and only God can do. We began the second volume by referring to these "God Things" as "God Kisses."

This third volume carries the same sentiment with the anticipation that God will touch people in areas that are as different as the stories themselves.

Hip. Hip. Hallelujah!

We Fed 5000
Be healed O Gulf of Mexico

It was mid-summer, 2010. On Memorial Day, a team of evangelical St. Bernard parish pastors motored out onto Lake Borgne and prayed together over the BP polluted waters of the Gulf of Mexico. We also shared the Lord's Supper and asked God for relief. It was my privilege to be a part of this small faith group.

Before we left we poured salt over the water, commemorating a biblical act of healing by the prophet Elisha. It was a powerful spiritual experience for all of us. I am thankful that I was there sharing the special time with genuine brothers in Christ.

Several weeks later our churches worked together again to distribute food to BP afflicted fishermen and their families. For several hours a long line of vehicles stretched nearly a mile alongside the highway waiting to receive their food boxes. We shook hands, prayed with each carload of people and when it was over we discovered that we had distributed food to 5000 people!

Some personal observations about feeding 5000 people.

First, when we hit that special "5000" number, unlike Jesus, we had nothing left over. Nothing. Not a single fragment.

Second, unlike Jesus, when we hit that special "5000" number, not only were we depleted of food, we were depleted of energy. We were worn out and exhausted.

Lastly, even though we had nothing left over and even though we were exhausted we discovered that each of our congregations are truly unbelievable people accomplishing the impossible for the glory of God!

Hip! Hip! Hallelujah!

A Gi-zillion Dollars!
He Owed A Debt He Could Not Pay!

"It ain't gonna happen," says he. "I'm five million in the red and there's no way out! It ain't gonna happen!"

The 1980s. That's when it happened. The American economy boomed then busted. No industry was harder hit then the housing industry; and, the man sitting across from my desk was upside down – in hock -- for five million dollars.

I was pastoring a small mission church at the time, simultaneously attending seminary, and also simultaneously working as a financial consultant for a firm in New Orleans.

If ever there was a man who owed a debt he could not pay – this was the man! We talked a lot, prayed a lot, and laid out a financial recovery plan. Slowly, very slowly, through a delicate process of buying, selling and refinancing the debt began to diminish.

There was, however, another debt he could not pay – his sin debt. In the midst of our strategy meetings he eventually received Christ. He invited Jesus into his heart and turned his will and life over to Christ. He discovered the truth of the old hymn, "Jesus paid it all, all to Him I owe."

After several months we hit a brick wall. His financial indebtedness was down to less than five hundred thousand dollars. He had restored his good name but could not find any wiggle room to maneuver what remained of his financial debt. His financial house of cards collapsed; but, he did not!

"Everyone experiences difficulties and I'm not exempt," said he. "If I've learned anything it is this -- Jesus of Nazareth, the Prince of Peace, gives unshakable peace and I've got that peace!"

Hip! Hip! Hallelujah!

Secret Love Letters?
A different kind of love story

"I loo-vee yoou, Bro-tho John," she whispered in my ear. "I loo-vee yoou, Bro-tho John," as she hugged me tightly, Sunday after Sunday.

I hold poignant, powerful memories of this very special woman. She loved God. She loved God's church and she loved me, God's pastor. Through her love, her pure genuine love, I learned valuable lessons about the joy of hugging.

Every Sunday she gave me her secret "love letters" – but I couldn't read a word that she had written – not a word. She would write these "love letters" over a period of several hours every Saturday, then, when she and only she knew that the letters were complete, she would roll them together tightly and wrap a brown rubber band around them.

In our world, too often people with Down syndrome are taken for granted and often overlooked by others. In reality, these special people are special gifts from God. They are some of God's greatest givers of love and of hugs! Someone once said, "If they ran the world, their ability to minister to others would not be wasted."

This special friend of mine is in heaven now. One day I'll see her again and we'll sit together and read those secret "love letters" – one by one.

Hip! Hip! Hallelujah!

A Little Bit At A Time
Progressive Revelation

He was less than a year old. And learning how to crawl. He would maneuver this way, then that. He was a genuine "rug rat." My son. My first born.

Learning to crawl is a key milestone in a baby's life. Crawling is a baby's first way of getting around by himself. It strengthens the muscles in preparation for walking. At about nine to ten months a baby will usually begin pushing off with his knees to get the boost needed to get mobile. And, goodness, my son was certainly mobile!

My wife and I were living in one of those old shotgun houses in New Orleans. The weather was turning cold and a big old match was taken from a large box of kitchen matches to light the open space gas heaters.

My son, our crawling toddler, a genuine explorer, was also very much attracted by the flickering flames of the open space heater. I was seated on the couch when suddenly my son bolted forward, crawling as fast as he could. He was totally fascinated by the colorful tongues of fire dancing inside of the open space heater.

Time was of essence as he rapidly scrawled on hands and knees toward the flickering tongues of fire.

"No! No! Stop! Stop! Quit! Quit! Burny! Burny!"

My son immediately stopped dead in his tracks at the sound of my excited, raised voice. He looked, first at me, then at the little flames dancing inside of the space heater. And, he learned his first fundamental lesson about fire – fire is hot. A basic lesson.

I did not explain to him the varying temperatures related to the various colors of flame. We did not have a conversation about the process of combustion. The reason we didn't is obvious – he was not ready for that type of information.

God works with us in a similar way, here a little, there a little, God moves us from one level of revelation to the next level, from strength to strength, from faith to faith, from glory to glory – and this is the work of the Spirit.

In like manner God's Truth is revealed by God progressively and is tailored to suit the needs of the person, time and place of the revelation. First, the milk of the Word of God, then the Meat, then the Strong Wine!

Hip! Hip! Ḥallelujah!

He Lives! He Lives Here!
Do you know who this man is?

Years ago, during my first pastorate, I attended a pastor's conference at the big First Baptist Church in Union, Mississippi. They had a special guest speaker, a prominent pastor who gave one of those "pastor to pastor" talks. He shared with us an experience he had earlier in his ministry, one that really spoke to me as a younger minister.

It seems that the pastor was walking down the long hallway of the early childhood department at his church. The church had a weekday preschool. At just the "right" moment a young mother came walking down the hall, holding the hand of her preschooler – a boy.

"Oh! Look," says she to her little boy as

she pointed toward the pastor, "look, do you know who that is?" The little boy looked at the pastor and said, "That's Jesus! He lives here!"

Years later, I was walking down the long hallway of the early childhood department at our church. We had a weekday preschool. At just the "right" moment a young mother came walking down the hall, holding the hand of her preschooler – a boy.

"Oh! Look," says she to her little boy as she pointed toward me, "look, do you know who that is?" The little boy looked at me and said, "That's Jesus! He lives here!"

Hip! Hip! Hallelujah!

Corny?
God will change your "want to's."

Someone, I don't remember who, once said when you get saved God will change your "want to's." When that happens many of the things you were once attracted to you suddenly avoid, and vice versa, many of the things you once avoided you're suddenly attracted to -- a sort of conversion of desire! This attraction/avoidance business is part of Christian growth.

As you grow and mature in faith, God "worketh in you both to will and to do His good pleasure" by changing your "want to's" -- your tastes and desires!

Now I've heard that sentiment repeated many times over the years, and, some of you have heard it too. Have you ever wondered, though, how far does this changed "want to" business go? We know by experience that the changed "want to" process operates in the context of spiritual choices, moral decisions and ethical concerns, emotional expression and other areas and arenas of our lives; but, what about....well, just how far does this changed "want to" business go?

"I hate corn on the cob," he said! "Some folks can't stomach spinach! Others can't tolerate asparagus! Me? I hate corn on the cob."

He was a friend, a brother in Christ and a fellow second year Bible college student; and, from the sound of things, not even God could change his "want to" when it came to corn on the cob! (But, I was mistaken!)

"Though I hate corn on the cob" says he, with a softening of his voice and a tear on the corner of each eye "for one hour God changed my hatred of corn on the cob into love!"

"Say what? How's that," I asked?

Things are sometimes financially tough and tight for married students with families who attend Bible college (and seminary too) and things were especially tough and tight for my friend, his wife and family. Like the old woman who lived in a shoe he and his wife had so many children (seven or eight), well, they didn't know what to do. The college, aware of the largeness of their family turned two of the married apartments into one to provide sufficient space. Like old Mother Hubbard, however, one day they went to the cupboard, and, well, the cupboard was bare – and so was his wallet and her purse!

"What to do? What to do," said chicken little who thought the sky was falling? "What to do? What to do," said he? "What to do? What to do," said the wife?

He drove around the small college town, worrying, wondering, and praying -- like chicken little he went to the King. Then, in the middle of a prayer, as he turned an old worn asphalt country road that led back to town he saw God's unusual answer to his prayer!

"A new chicken shack drive thru restaurant was opening that very day," says he, and one of the grand opening activities was a good ole Mississippi corn-on-the-cob eating contest with the winner receiving a fresh, brand-new, hot off the press, genuine one hundred dollar bill."

Somewhere in the midst of this memory I hear a faint encouraging echo from the Word of God: "God shall supply all your need!"

(Count on it!) "Every good and perfect gift (even corn-on-the-cob) comes from God" (Count on it!)

Now, let me ask again -- just how far does this changed "want to" business go? Just wondering!

Hip! Hip! Hallelujah!

The Notion....?
Took a notion? Hmmmm. Was it really?

I was doing Vacation Bible School follow-up visitation when I "took a notion" to go visit Joe. He had terminal cancer and only a few weeks to live. As I rang the doorbell Joe's wife Yvonne came to the door.

"How did you know," she asked? "Know what," I asked? "Joe just died less than two minutes ago. I haven't even called my children!"

"Took a notion?" Hmmmm. Was it really? Walking with God? Hmmmm. If so, well, there was no thunder from heaven. No earthquake. No angelic host. It was just a notion. Just a notion? Was it really?

Hip. Hip, Hallelujah!

The Box…..?
Everything I have is in this box.

His name was Robert. As he got into my car I asked, "What's in the box?"

"My stuff," says he as we headed for the train station.

Some folks would say he was a simpleton! I wasn't too sure about that; but, he did have limited social skills or some type of psychological disorder. And now, well, his mom had died, he had no money other than a small government disability check and …he was being evicted. The train would get him safely to Kentucky. Kin folks lived there, or so he said.

As we quietly drove along I recalled some of our previous conversations, conversations we had when he was not so heavily medicated. His hands would shake as he talked about life – his life – and love, or the absence of love. Beneath what everyone saw, he was, well, a real man, an ordinary guy, just like you and just like me.

"Your stuff," I asked? "Is that it?" "Yes, sir, that's my stuff. Everything I have. It's in this box. Thankful too!"

"Want me to stay with you till the train comes," I asked as we pulled into the station.

"Naw," says he, "I want to smoke some cigarettes. He was a chain smoker, big time.

As I drove off he stood in the middle of the station, holding his box, smoking cigarettes. That was the last time I saw him, simply standing there holding his box.

Years later. 2005. Katrina. I led a small group in worship at First Baptist Church, Chalmette, then quickly drove home. My wife had just finished packing several boxes in our automobile. We hopped into the car and evacuated.

Several hours later we arrived safely at my daughters place. I unloaded several boxes filled with stuff my wife had packed.

"That last one, over there, in the car… that one's yours," says she.

I asked, "What in the box?"

"Your stuff," says she.

"My stuff?"

As I stood there holding the box I saw a faint reflection of myself in the car window.

"Robert?"

Thank I heard what sounded like a distant voice.

"Thankful too!"

Hip. Hip, Hallelujah!

In Hot Water
And it was cold too!

It was cold! Dead of the winter Mississippi cold! The Church of God pastor had two candidates for Baptism – but no baptismal!

"We normally use the pond," says he, "but its way too cold for that!"

So, the following Saturday evening I put the giant burners on to heat the cold waters of our baptismal.

The plan? Baptize their two candidates in between our two Sunday services. One problem! The giant burners were just that –giant! No technology here – just turn it on, let 'er heat up, then turn it off! Easy, right? Not quite. Saturday night I hit the sack and completely forgot that the giant burners were heating up the baptismal waters.

Sunday morning. Early. The church building was filled with the sound of bubbling waters and steam – I mean steam as if in a steam-filled sauner. I opened every window, opened every door and drained half the water from the sauner-baptismal – then refilled the tank with cold water.

Well, our church dismissed…the Church of God came…and the baptisms proceded…sort of. The first candidate was the preacher's son. One thing, before I finish this story…hot water rises to the top. The poor preacher's kid was shivering below the belt and gettin' as red as a crawfish up above. Beads of sweat were pouring off his head.

"Its hot, daddy. Its cold, daddy."

"Be quiet boy," said the preacher under his breath. He was hot and cold too!

The daddy dunked the boy and the sanctuary filled with the guttural growl of the boy as he went under the water. He came out with a muffled scream and a yelp. So too did the lady that followed.

One thing I could never figure out about this whole episode. The Church of God preacher never did call to use our baptismal again. Go figure!

Hip. Hip. Hallelujah!

Alone In The World!
A Broken Hallelujah

Alone! I conducted a funeral today – for a man I did not know! And, it appears, no one else knew him either. He was alone! Alone in the world! No family. No friends. Never married. Alone. All alone.

He was originally from St. Bernard. But, he bounced around the country – alone – and died in Florida. Poor. Broke. Alone. Two friends from long ago, a husband and wife, who lived in in Missouri heard about his death; and it broke their hearts to know that he was alone, all alone in the world.

The couple traveled to Florida, had the body shipped to St. Bernard, covered the expenses of the funeral. They flew down to attend, and mourned and wept as they fully realized the plight of this long ago friend, a friend who was alone, all alone, in life and at the moment of his death.

Gilbert O'Sullivan once sang a song, in the 60's I believe, titled "Alone Again, Naturally" that focused on how easy it is for us to isolate and be alone. God said in His Word that this is not good: "It is not good for man to be alone."

In the movie "It's A Wonderful Life" there is a line that is spoken to George Bailey. He was in a crisis and felt alone, all alone. The line? "A man who has friends is never alone!"

The best friend you can ever have is sitting in a Bible study class in a church near you. God has fixed things so that you never need to be alone! Hope to see you Sunday, in the church of God's choice.

A Broken Hallelujah

The Man Who Did What?
This story makes me smile

11:30 p.m. "Can you come?" says the voice on the other end of the phone. "He won't make it through the night!" Thirty minutes later we met in the front room of her home. A hospital bed filled the room. On it was a man, her husband. Tubes, wires, and machines were everywhere.

"He's not saved," says she. "And he's going to die tonight!"

"One other thing," says she. He's completely paralyzed. He can't talk or move – he can't even squeeze your hand or finger."

I bent over the hospital bed and began sharing Christ, slowly whispering God's plan of salvation into his ear. I closed my share time with him by leading him in that special prayer of faith and repentance, urging him to invite Christ into what remained of his life.

"Do you think he invited Christ into his life," says she.

"I'm going to try to find out," says me.

"Mister, I know you can't talk and I know you can't even squeeze my hand, but I noticed while we were praying that your lip quivered and moved, just a tad. Sir, if you invited Christ into your life – if you can, would you smile.!"

Unbelievably, he flashed one of the biggest, sweetest smiles I think I'd ever seen. Before sunrise, he died. I call him the man who smiled his way into heaven.

Sometimes, things seem hopeless. Sometimes, it seems as if all is lost. The key word is "seems" – what "seems" to be is not always what is. The world of appearances is often deceptive. So, be patient. Trust God….. and smile!

Hip. Hip. Hallelujah

This Little Piggy
A Different Kind Of Love Story!

He was a pig farmer; and he was drunk… shouting obscenities, cussing and waving a pistol every which way as he stepped into my church office.

"I'm gonna blow his blanky-blank head off!" shouted he at the top of his lungs. "I'm gonna blow his blanky-blank head off, I tell you…blow his blanky-blank head off!"

Somehow (by the grace of God) I was able to calm him down. His story? His son had gotten him drunk and had the ole pig farmer sign the title deed to the pig farm over to the son. Then, the son , after filing the necessary papers, promptly had the ole man evicted.

"I'm gonna blow his blanky-blank head off!" shouted he to the top of his lungs. "I'm gonna blow his blanky-blank head off, I tell you…blow his blanky-blank head off!"

He agreed to wait a day and allow me the opportunity to talk with the son. I did and had no success, none whatsoever. The son was as hard as nails.

Then, the next day came….
"I'm gonna blow his blanky-blank head off!" shouted he to the top of his lungs. "I'm gonna blow his blanky-blank head off, I tell you… blow his blanky-blank head off!"

His old pick-up truck kicked dust and gravel everywhere as he left the church parking lot. I called the sheriff's office as a precaution. About twenty minutes later, with lights flashing and sirens blaring, an ambulance passed by, headed in the same direction as the ole pig farmer.

"Oh! No! Dear God! He's killed his son!" But, he hadn't. About ½ a mile down the highway he had flipped his pickup! The back wheel was still spinning when I got there!

"He had a stroke!" said the emergency room doctor. When I saw him the next day his face was contorted. His arm shriveled with his hand near his chin. He couldn't see, He couldn't speak.

"He probably can't hear, either," said the doctor.

Day after day for nearly two weeks I whispered God's plan of salvation in his ear, always closing the prayer by saying, "Ask Jesus to come to you, and He will. Ask Him in your head to come into your heart. Talk to Him in your head."

One day I was completely caught off guard and startled. As I finished praying over him the ole pig farmer's twisted, contorted arm suddenly reached toward me. Grabbing my neck he pulled my head toward his face. With a raspy voice he said, "Go tell my son about Jesus! Tell my son I love him and God loves him too!

Two days later he died!

Think about it! Lost people don't tell other people about Jesus. Only saved people do that!

Hip. Hip. Hallelujah

Will Work For Food!
Behind the cardboard sign - Part 1

A man holds up a cardboard sign: WILL WORK FOR FOOD! You see them everywhere; people begging for money with signs reading 'Homeless,' 'Out of work vet,' or 'Will work for food.' But what are the stories behind the cardboard signs. Here's one!

"I saw you sitting here and the Lord led me to pull over," says I.

Strange how God works, isn't it? Strange. "Do you have a church home, a church family, a pastor?" I asked.

"Boy, I must look terrible," says he – and he did. He looked more like a human skeleton than a man. His clothes were grimy. His hair was matted. He was a mess, a real mess.

"Brother John, its me (and then he said his name). I was shocked.

I hadn't seen him since hurricane Katrina….and, now here he was, in such terrible shape, so terrible that I did not recognize him – a beggar and a pan handler, begging for food.

An ancient proverb says that "first the man takes the drink, then the drink takes the man." His alcoholism had taken him, al"right" , it had taken him where he never thought he would be – homeless, hopeless, a beggar and a pan handler on the rough streets of the city of New Orleans.

We talked awhile – about life, about his predicament, about the old days, and about Christ and His wonder working power – and we prayed, oh, how we prayed.

"There is a way out of this," I shared, "there is a way through. If I never see you again, if you forget everything I've said, remember this – even now, God still has a wonderful plan for you and for your life. As an old hymn says, "It is no secret what God can do; what He's done for others He'll do for you!"

As we parted I promised him a miracle. My wife says I always promise people miracles. Well, I'm guilty. I promised him a miracle – and, God did that miracle! He was in church the following Sunday.

Will Work For Food!
Behind the cardboard sign - Part 2

Some Helpful Keys To Recovery

ADMIT you have a problem and that you are powerless over alcohol/drugs and that your life is unmanageable (A bigger task than you might think. Lay down your denial, forget justifying your drinking/using, and stop blaming others – admit you have a problem!)

ACKNOWLEDGE that others, who were just as powerless as you, if not more so, have found a power outside of themselves that restored them to sanity

ACQUIESCE by turning your will and your life over to Jesus Christ, the only Power that can truly set you free.

ACTION is needed at some point – begin by sweeping your own sidewalk. Make a fierce searching moral inventory of the wrongs you have done, the hurts you have caused and the pain you have afflicted.

AMMENDS need to be made, do it! If you need guidance on how to do this – get it! Humble yourself!

AVOIDANCE is necessary -- Change your Playmates, your Playgrounds, and your Playthings. (Don't box yourself in by thinking you can bring recovery to your old friends – it's a trap!)

ALLIANCE Once you turn your will and life over to Christ there is an alliance made between you and God. In this new alliance there is a part that is God's that you cannot do (God will do His part! Count on it!) and there is a part that is yours that God will not do (Do your part! Sit on your hands! You can't put a drink to your lips or shoot anything into your body – if you sit on your hands! Do it! Do your part and watch God do His part!)

AWARENESS of the negative influence of H.A.L.T. is necessary If you're Hungry, Angry, Lonely, or Tired – H.A.L.T -- do your part! Hungry? Then eat! Angry? Calm down. Call your pastor, your mentor, or a brother in Christ! Lonely? Meet with someone, someone you respect, someone you trust. Call a friend. Call your pastor. Call your Bible class teacher. Get out of the house. Don't allow loneliness take you down! Tired? Get some rest! This Too Shall Pass!

ALERTNESS is necessary. Be alert to the fact that you can actually SABOTAGE your own recovery. In the back of your mind there is a Sabotage Mechanism with a "hair-trigger" that will make you think you can't deal with life or a life crisis without a drink or assistance from a mood-altering chemical! You are surrounded by millions of people who deal with life and life crisis' without chemicals! You can do this!

Enough Said!
        Hip! Hip! Hallelujah!

Black Rocks
Take my photograph!

It was the middle of June! No AC! No money! The First Baptist Church of Chalmette's Grand Opening was slated for mid-September!

"Shut it down!" said the hurricane Katrina construction recovery leadership.

"Not yet!" says I.

My stomach was in knots and my faith was weak as I left the meeting.

"There he is. He's the pastor," shouted a group of construction volunteers, pointing toward me. A short black man, a man I had never met, stepped from the crowd and spoke directly to me.... with a strange-sounding British accent -- his name was Charles!

"I too am a pastor. God told me to stop

many times as I drove by your church, but I did not. I cannot explain why I did not! I just did not! Today, however, the Holy Spirit MADE me stop. Pastor, God MADE me stop and He told me I MUST pray with you and I MUST give you a message -- He will build your church!"

A Word from God! A Word through a strange-sounding West African pastor, thousands of miles away from his homeland! I was stunned! A desperately needed Word from God -- "God will build your church!" Before we prayed he showed me a photo of his childhood church in W. Africa. "When I was a boy," says he, "I and the other children would carry black rocks up the mountain to build a new church. This is a photo of that church."

It was a church made of beautiful "black rock." A second photograph had nearly a hundred W. African boys and girls standing in front of the "black rock" church.

"And these are the 'living stones,' pastor –remember God's message – He will build your church!"

The following week 70 or 80 construction volunteers came from Chattanooga, Tennessee. I told many stories to the group and ended by telling the story of Charles, the West

African pastor, and the "black rock." The volunteers from Chattanooga were stunned into silence as I mentioned the "black rock." Nearly a dozen rushed forward and placed a small "black rock" in my hand.

"Our pastor," says one, "gave each of us several 'black rocks' -- prayer rocks, he called them -- before we came on this mission trip to help rebuild your church. He told us that God would let us know exactly who should get our 'black rocks.' God just let us know -- you, pastor, are to have our 'black rocks.' Keep it in your pocket. We will pray for you. God will build your church."

About four weeks later the same church in Chattanooga sent nearly a dozen AC technicians to "hook up" our AC – just in time for the grand opening.

Today, there are folks across the country and in our church who have one of my little "black rocks" in their pockets or purses! Why? Because there is a God and He hears and answers our prayer!

Hip! Hip! Hallelujah!

Mack
A man, not a truck

Back when I made my decision to receive Christ, four other men walked the church aisle as well. James and I became pastors. Al and another fine Christian, also named John, eventually became deacons. However, one of the five, Mack, didn't continue in the faith.

Unfortunately, through distance and the passage of time, I've lost track of Mack. I have, however, wondered about him often. I've prayed for him often.

You see, for some reason Mack simply didn't persevere. Perhaps he was like Demas (1 Tm.4:10) and loved the world more than he loved Christ. Or perhaps, like one of the seeds in the parable of the sower, he lacked something necessary to perseverance (Matt.13:18-22).

I imagine if you look carefully you can find a 'Mack' or two in your past too. They once stood tall for Christ but now, well, they're no where to be found.

Nearly thirty years ago when I began my pastoral ministry at First Baptist Church, Chalmette, a church leader shared his concerns with me about people who fall away.

"When I first got saved," says he, "I was given a copy of a workbook called 'The Survival Kit' for new believers. When I read that title, I thought to myself – I might not survive!"

I wonder about him too! Like Mack, he is no where to be found.

I read an article in a Christian magazine a number of years ago. The title of the article – "Saved By Christ – Lost To The Church!" While you think about these things, be careful. Make sure you're not a Mack! Be careful, you just might not survive! Without Jesus you cannot do anything!

Thank God for Jesus, His Unspeakable Gift
Hip! Hip! Hallelujah!

The Puzzle
Puzzled By A Puzzling Puzzle

Christmas! A long, long time ago! I must have been 8 or 9 yrs old. My family was into puzzles back then! The Christmas presents were unwrapped. Things had settled down. I was on the floor putting together the pieces of the big, giant, 1000 piece puzzle. Next to me was my brother, Glenn. He was two years younger than I. Before him on the floor were the pieces of a giant 500 piece puzzle. Across the room my baby sister, Terry, was working with one of those toddler puzzles. It had only 4 or 5 pieces – squares, circles, triangles, and stuff like that. (Sorry, Kelly and Scott, you weren't born yet).

Every now and then my baby sister Terry would get puzzled by her puzzle. She was learning that squares do not fit into circles and rectangles didn't fit into triangles.

Totally absorbed in my puzzle I became frustrated as my concentration was suddenly and quickly broken. The source? My brother, Glenn.

"Hey," says he, "Where does this go?" Needless to say I wasn't a happy camper. Here's the deal: Glenn, puzzled by his puzzling puzzle, wanted help with his puzzling puzzle – from me! Yes! From me! And, that wasn't going to happen!

You see – I was so puzzled by my own puzzling puzzle that I didn't have time to help Glenn or anyone else who was puzzled by their puzzling puzzle! I was just too puzzled by my puzzling puzzle to un-puzzle anyone else's puzzling puzzle! Puzzling, isn't it?

Isn't life sometimes like that! Puzzled by the puzzle of our puzzling life we turn for help and guidance – usually to others who are just as puzzled by their puzzling puzzles as we are!

Years have passed since that puzzling Christmas experience. I've discovered that new puzzles constantly crop up – life puzzles that need to be solved! It's that way for all of us!

Someone reading this is puzzled about raising a difficult child! Someone else is puzzled by how to restore the fire in your marriage! Someone else, is puzzled about how to overcome financial difficulties!

What's puzzling you? And, where do you go? And, where do you turn when you're puzzled by your puzzling puzzle?

> Hint #1 -- If you need wisdom, ask our generous God, and He will give it to you. He will not rebuke you for asking. But when you ask Him, be sure that your faith is in God and God alone. [James 1:5-6].

> Hint #2 – Trust GOD from the bottom of your heart; don't try to figure out everything on your own. Listen for GOD's voice in everything you do, everywhere you go; He's the one who will keep you on track. [Proverbs 3:5 The Message]

> Hint #3 -- [Jesus said] "…without Me you can do nothing! [John 15:5]

Hip! Hip! Hallelujah!

The Instant Celebrity
A Mathematical Ignoramus!

If a man proclaims that he's an agnostic, he's given a book contract, appears on talk radio, and late night television – in essence he's given a platform to tell the world he's an agnostic! Strange, at least in my estimation. You see the word "agnostic" is derived from the Latin word "ignoramus!"

Imagine that, a man proclaims that he's an "ignoramus" and boom –he's an instant media celebrity!

I was visiting the locked ward of a psychiatric hospital when a male patient in a straight jacket called out my name. "John! John! John!"

I was shocked to see a fella from my elementary school years. "What are you doing here," I asked, "What are you doing here?" With tears in his eyes he said, "John. John. It's terrible! It's terrible! I don't know math, John. I don't know math. I'm a mathematical ignoramus, John. I'm a mathematical ignoramus."

Think about this a bit. If a man proclaims he is a "mathematical ignoramus" – he's locked up in a psychiatric ward. If a man proclaims he is a "God ignoramus" – well, read the opening paragraph.

Left - Right! Left - Right!
Wait..What..Where?

In life, there are people who share our journey. There are also special people who not only share our journey but shape us in ways that are deep and profound! It seems to be woven into the fabric of life that we help and influence others and others in turn help and influence us. Our lives are largely constructed using bricks handed to us by others. Even the mortar that keeps everything together – given to us!

Which brings me to Nathaniel. Nathaniel's one of my six grandchildren. When Nathaniel was 3 yrs/4 yrs old he was securely seated in the back seat of my car – headed to Happy Paw Paw's house (Happy Paw Paw – that's me).

"There's an airplane, Happy Paw Paw!

There's an airplane over there!"

"Where?"

"There, over there, Happy Paw Paw, over there!"

I must have been looking the wrong way out of the wrong window. I didn't see the airplane.

":No, Happy Paw Paw, over there!" (Nathaniel was getting frustrated with me!)

"Where?":

It became obvious that Nathaniel did not yet know the difference between "right" and "left"– so a fundamental life lesson began. Nothing profound. Nothing deep. But knowing the difference between "right" and "left" is an essential lesson that Nathaniel needed to learn and carry throughout life.

"This is my "left" hand, This is my "right" hand. This is my "left"" ear. This is my "right" ear. This is the "left" window. This is the "right" window." On and on we went – then came that miraculous moment – "Do you still see the airplane, Nathaniel? Where is the airplane, Nathaniel?"

"Its over there, Happy Paw Paw. It's on the"left" side. Look through the"left" window!"

Mission Accomplished, sort of. You know and I know that there were and still are many life lessons for Nathaniel to learn. He's a teenager now! (Another story)

But, what about you? (And, what about me?) In life, there are people who have shared and are sharing our journey; and, like everyone else there are some special people who have not only shared but have shaped us in ways that are deep and profound!

I doubt that Nathaniel remembers or realizes that Happy Paw Paw taught him the vital distinction between "left" and "right". But, the shadow of Happy Paw Paw will always remain – hidden in the past as the one who shared a simple, yet essential life lesson that shaped Nathaniel.

Think for a moment. Who is back there, hidden in the past, perhaps unseen, standing in the shadows of your life? And, who is under the shadow of your life? While learning the difference between left and "right" is essential – there are some bigger issues at play here!

Things like "Rejoice" or "Regret" -- because of WHO or WHAT lingers in the shadows! Enough Said!

Hip. Hip. Hallelujah!

Buddy And The PhD!
A different sort of evangelism

Buddy. His name was Buddy; and, he was everybody's friend. He loved God. He loved people. He loved the lost. That's why when the church announced a special evangelism class that would teach participants how to share there faith, well, Buddy was the first to sign up!

We began training on a Friday night. Praying together. Sharing together. Role playing. Memorizing Scripture. Learning how to use soul-winning tracks and how to share our story. And, we learned more, so much more! It was great. Wonderful. And, Buddy was vibrant, alive and in the middle of everything. He had trouble with the memory work and did the best, the very best that he could; and, he loved it.

On Saturday morning, more training and prayer time; then, we received visitation assignments. It was now time to go into "the highways and byways" -- Discover! Develop! Deploy! We had Discovered God's Plan of Salvation; Developed A Strategy To Share God's Plan of Salvation; and, now, we were ready to Deployed!

Then came our final instructions as visitation assignments were handed out: "No matter who you are assigned to visit – Do not! I repeat, Do not! Do not trade your assignment with anyone else! The Holy Spirit chose the people that are assigned to you. Do not trade your assignments with anyone else!"

There was a hush as the assignments were distributed. Here's why. Everybody's friend, Buddy, was probably the least educated among the group. He dropped out of school in the sixth grade. Buddy couldn't read. He could barely sign his name. And, his assignments? Two professors of philosophy on the staff of Tulane University!

The next day was Sunday! The church was packed. Wonderful Music! Great Preaching! Then, the most exciting part – the invitation! Everyone was eager to see the results of our training. People were receiving Christ, coming forward. The invitation was about to close when…

………two professors of philosophy from Tulane University came forward to profess faith in Christ. They had turned from Something – their Sin! And, they had turned to Someone – their Savior.

"Buddy came to visit," one of the professors shared later, "We talked a bit when suddenly Buddy said, in the midst of our conversation, 'Hey! Listen! I'm not as smart as you guys and I can't even remember what I trained to say; but, I want you to know that I asked Jesus into my heart and my life two years ago and he changed me. He saved me. And He changed my life. And, He will save you and change your life too!' Then he prayed with us and prayed for us."

Soul Winning Training?
Take it! Learn how!
But, in the end – remember, it's not what you know, its WHO you follow!
Share Your Story!
Discover! Develop! Deploy!
Hip. Hip. Hallelujah!

In The Trash Can
Throw-Away People! Not Me!

He was my pastor! And, he was about to make a big mistake! But, the Holy Spirit would not let him! And, boy, am I glad pastor didn't make that mistake!

Think about it! Some people collect baseball cards! Others, collect football cards! Pastor's collect Church Visitor Cards! You know, the kind of card that visitors to your church fill out when they visit the church. That's the kind of cards pastor's collect.

Now, I don't know what folks do with old baseball cards, or old football cards. I guess they put 'em away in a drawer, trade 'em or sell 'em – or, perish the thought – throw 'em away!

Well, old Church Visitor Cards are like

that too, sort of! You see, Church Visitor Cards are stored for safe keeping. A good pastor will visit the person whose info is on the Church Visitor Card – and move the card to the Membership File when the person gets saved and unites with the church.

But, not everyone unites with the church; and, old Church Visitor Cards begin to pile up. First, you have one stack, then two, then, well, you get the idea. Sometimes, the pastor will accumulate so many cards that he feels that he must throw some of them away.

Such was the case of my pastor (or, soon to be pastor at the time of this incident). You see, every year my pastor would "clean" his stack of cards. And, as he would often tell the story, he would come "to the Church Visitor Card for this guy, John Jeffries, and I'd throw it into the waste can. This Jeffries guy will never get saved." Then, says he, "The Holy Spirit said, 'Give 'em one more year!" And, he did!

This happened three times over a two year period. My pastor would throw me away and the Holy Spirit would convince him to pull me out of that waste can, for just a little longer.

Through the years I've encouraged my ministerial, mission and administrative staff to see each card as a person. Why? Because there are no "Throw Away-People!" Nope! Not a one!

Hip. Hip. Hallelujah!

A Guardian Angel!
An 18-Wheeler! And -- Yipes!

There's one thing my wife hates, simply hates! Nope, make that two! Number one on her hate list is driving behind an 18-wheeler.

"They take up the whole road and ya can't see a thing! Nothing!"

The second thing that she abhors is driving in rainy weather!

"It's dangerous," says she, "simply dangerous! I hate it when it rains while I'm driving, simply hate it!"

So, imagine this! We're heading to a wedding in Tennessee driving up I-49 outside of Shreveport, Louisiana. I'd already driven a stretch so now she's behind the wheel. We're in the left lane and – a flash of lightening, a clap of thunder – and rain, rain everywhere

My wife switched lanes moving into the slower right lane!

The wife slows down.

"This is dangerous," says she, "simply dangerous! I hate it when it rains while I'm driving, simply hate it!"

The windshield wipers were going back and forth, back and forth, flop, flop, flop, flop….and then. finally, the rain began slowing to a drizzle.

"Now what in the world is he doing," I heard the wife say.

I mean, goodness, there arose such a clatter I abruptly turned to see, what was the matter, when there through the window, what should I see – an 18-wheeler driving, driving as fast as can be!

"They take up the whole road and ya can't see….," says she.

As the 18-wheeler, driving in the left lane, began to catch up with us my heart nearly jumped out of my throat. There, across the median on I-49 in the southbound lane, was a pick-up truck whose driver had lost complete control of his vehicle.

As he rumbled uncontrollably across the median it was obvious that we were going to have a head on collision, when….

….at just the last minute the 18-wheeler

came between us and the out-of-control pick-up.

All any of us –the driver of the pick-up, the trucker and my wife and I – all any of us could do was hold on….. Boom, blap, blap, blap, boom, boom.

"He hit us," says the wife. "The 18-wheeler hit us!"

We pulled over, the wife did, and the trucker in his 18-wheeler, he pulled over too!

The driver in the out of control pick-up amazingly had turned at just the last minute, completely missing the 18-wheeler, then drove completely across our north-bound lane into a deep ditch. When we finally came to a stop the pick up, unscathed, was about ½ mile behind us.

"Did I hit you?" asked the trucker as he stepped from his 18-wheeler. "Did I hit you?"

Along the back fender of our car was a small ripple.

"Yes. Well, sort of, but, we're in safe hands."

"Oh," says he. "Yes, I have that insurance too!"

"Not talking about insurance," says I pointing to heaven. "Not talking about insurance!"

"Oh! Gotcha," says he. "I'm a Christian too!"

Enough Said!
Hip! Hip! Hallelujah!

Shirts that Talk!
But What Are They Saying!

Amazing! Across from me standing in line at a local convenience store was a man and a woman, obviously a husband and a wife. Both wore matching tee shirts with coordinated writing on the front and back of their shirts. Behind the couple was man, a man with a big belly half hanging out and over his blue jeans. He too had a tee shirt with writing on the his shirt, but only on the front, with the writing stretched tightly from side to side.

Now I'm convinced that at least a couple of life messages can be found through these tee shirts. Just wondering. What do you think? Can you put together some life messages.

The first couple – the old guy, the husband, had a shirt that said "Old Grouch" and his wife wore a matching shirt that said "Old Grouch's Wife." The second guy, who really was out of shape wore a tee shirt that said "I Wish I'd Known I'd Be Here This Long – I'd Have Taken Better Care Of Myself"

Shirts that Talk!
But What Are They Saying!

Enough Said!
Hip! Hip! Hallelujah!

Little Boys, Tall Trees
And Axes!

There were three of us, yes sir, there were three. Little Boys! We were good boys too! Why, we even had "merit badges" to prove it. And we were taught to always "Be Prepared."

Yes sir, there were three of us. We were part of a larger group of boys, just like us…. Little boys, good boys….put us all together and we were a Troop – a Boy Scout Troop. And, all of us were on one of those special trips in the great wilderness called St. Tammany parish in Louisiana, just above Covington, to be exact – near the Village of Folsom.

We three, did I tell you, we were good boys, well, yes, of course we were, we were good boys because Boy Scouts are always good and always live by that special motto – "Be Prepared!"

Well, we three were in the thick of the wilderness, away from the troop, working our way through the forest. We were surrounded by tall pine trees – and no telling what else! Lions? Bears? Tigers? Indians? Who knows what lurked in those woods?

Well, one of us, certainly not me, came up with a bright idea – we need to be prepared – so, let's cut down this tall pine tree then, after it falls, we can be prepared and make our own secret hideout! Good idea. We all agreed. To this day it surprises me when I recall how quickly three good little boys chopped down that pine tree. I mean the tree was at least thirty-forty or perhaps a thousand feet tall.

Before you know it --- faloom – down came the tree – with a loud, loud roar – faloom!! Scared the heart out of us! Now, I don't know what was hiding in those woods, but we three good boys started running every which way as loud angry voices were getting closer and closer to us – and to the fallen tree. It might have been an Indian, or an angry farmer with a pitchfork, I don't know who or what it was. I was just too, too busy running, running, running, as fast as I could to get away from that tree.

Later that night, around the camp fire, the troop leader told stories about trees, tall trees, and forests, thick forests and he told us about private property too – and he told us about how little boys with axes could be dangerous, even to tall trees in the forests. (Even Smoky the Bear was concerned about trees and forests, says he!) Then, he told everyone about THE tree. Every one was silent as he told about THE tree. Sweat was rolling down my face, my neck and my back. (Momma once said she had an eye in the back of her head – she didn't say that troop leaders had them too!) And then, he called all three of us good little boys before the troop, I mean the whole troop. And, I wondered, as I stood there sweating, sweating, and sweating some more -- how did he know?

The Bible says,
> "Be sure your sin will find you out!"
>
> (Numbers 32:23)

Hip! Hip! Hallelujah!

Always Be Ready
He "Out-Hooked" The Hooker!

A man of God was walking down a long airport ramp with a small suitcase swinging back and forth, back and forth, with each step he took as he left the airport for the "Big Easy" – New Orleans!

The Bible says that we should "always be ready to give an explanation to anyone…" – but, this was ridiculous!

As he reached the bottom of the ramp she seemingly stepped out of no where. He was startled. Her appearance, the way she dressed and her seductive manner left no doubt about her intention. Her approach initially caught him off guard.

"The hooker raised her balled fist into the air and held it in front of my face! On her fist she had drawn two eyes with long eye lashes. A circle of lipstick painted around her curled up thumb and forefinger gave the appearance of ruby red lips."

"Hello, big boy," says she. "Wanta have some fun?"

"Wait a minute," says he. He put his suitcase down and reached into his inside coat pocket and pulled out a marks-a-lot. He drew two eyes and a mustache on his hand, then, held it in front of her face! She smiled, thinking they were going to play a game – not so!

"Hello," says he. "Young lady if you were to die tonight would you open your eyes in heaven?"

He "Out-Hooked" The Hooker!

"Won another one that night," said he. "Won another one that night!"

Hip. Hip. Hallelujah!

Come Please!
The Angel Of Death!

"Come, please! Please come! Come before night!"

His voice was frantic, filled with fright – fearful! He and his wife had attended but not joined the church years earlier, and, now – they were in a thick of trouble!

"I don't know if she's insane or on the verge of insanity – something's wrong! Come, please! Please come! Come before night!"

Later – mid-afternoon – I went to their home. I saw her before she saw me! I was at the bottom of a curved stairwell as she carefully and cautiously started down. She had aged since I'd last seen her – about five months earlier.

She was startled when she first saw me! Instinctively, she drew a quick, deep breath and just as quickly drew her hand to her chest! Then – her eyes – she was dealing with a greater fear!

"What are you looking for," says I?

"He's not here yet," says she. "He usually comes at night! But, you never know! He may come tonight! You never know!"

She spoke hesitantly about her fears, about her anxieties and about a little graveyard next to a now abandoned white clapboard church.

"I must get out of here, while it is day. I must, I must have air!"

Centuries ago, Christians sometimes celebrated a believer's death as his "birthday" – their day of entry into heaven! They celebrated because they believed what the Bible had to say about death, i.e., Christ has delivered His children from the fear of death – and we no longer need to live in bondage to that fear (Hebrews 2:14-15). They understood (and believed) that "death had no sting and the grave had no victory!" (1 Corinthian 15:55).

A broken moon spilled through two large oaks in front of their home. A flush of pink and red azaleas danced as gentle twisting winds blew. It was later that night. I had returned, as promised. She was on her couch, which was strategically placed so that she could see both the front and back first floor entrances to her home. She had somehow come to believe that when the Angel of Death came – he would come through either the front or back entrance. She had so positioned herself that if he came in the front, she would escape through the back; and vice versa.

She disbelieved Scripture – disregarded its sufficiency – and rejected all attempts to help her. I lost touch with them and never heard from them in the aftermath of hurricane Katrina.

What about you? What about me? Can we conquer our fear of death? Everyone must eventually battle fear! Some fear heights. Others fear flying. Still others fear drowning, or snakes, or mice. Everyone has a fear of death. No one is immune. Fear of death, however, can actually paralyze a person – grip and hold us -- such as the lady who feared the Angel of Death.

Can we conquer our fear of death? It depends on who the "we" is referred to in this question.

If you are numbered with the unsaved, the lost and you are not born again -- you should fear death. As written in Hebrews 10:31, "It is a fearful thing to fall into the hands of the living God."

If you are numbered with the saved, the redeemed and you are born again – you have nothing to fear. David understood that he had nothing to fear when he wrote, "Even though I walk through the valley of the shadow of death, I will fear no evil, for you are with me." (Psalm 23:4) Paul understood this too. He writes to young Timothy (and to you – and to me). He wants us to know that "… God has not given us a spirit of fear…"

Paul could sleep peacefully, night or day, with the thought that the Angel of Death could come for him at any time… And you can sleep peacefully too! And so can I! And so can that lady – through faith in and assurance from Christ! He is our peace!

Hip. Hip. Hallelujah!

The Rhinestone Cowboy
The Great Cow Stampede

"Daddy! Daddy! There's a cowboy outside! There's a cowboy outside!"

"And a bunch of cows too, Daddy – a bunch of cows!"

I quickly got up from the couch (football game!) and raced to the front door -- in my sock feet – no shoes! No boots! Just me and my sock feet. (City boy – Remember?)

Cowboy? Nope. Not a single cowboy. Didn't see a single one! Just ole man MacElleny – he lived down the road a piece! I can see him even now – denim overalls, red and black checkered flannel shirt – and his long white hair and beard just blowin' in the wind.

Ole man MacElleny was running as fast as

he could, huffin' and puffin' – just running as fast as he could. What a sight!

Sure enough, there were cows – a whole herd of cows – well, not exactly – a lil bit less than a dozen. But, by golly, I'd never seen anything like this back in New Orleans, no sir, never did -- it was (in my mind) a genuine stampede! And those cows (yipes!), they were running toward me! I mean, right toward me!

"Help me out, preacher! Help me out," yelled MacElleny, "Help me out!"

The ole, out-of-breath cowboy (MacElleny) was runnin' as fast as he could, trying to corral his runaway cows! I mean he was huffin' and puffin' – huffin' and puffin' – runnin' as fast as he could.

"Help me out, preacher! Help me out!"

With more ignorance than courage I began to run (in sock feet, mind you) with arms spread wide open, trying to scare the runaway cows -- yelling my dang head off! Don't recall what I was saying! Don't know what the heck I was trying to do! I was just there, in my sock feet, running, sort of tiptoeing fast-like, kicking my knees up high, looking like a "girlie girl" -- yelling my dang head off tryin' to head off the herd of stampeding cows!

Then it came, thank God – it came! My epiphany! (epiphany – when a light bulb comes on inside your head!) God's been known to do that, you know! Sure enough!

"Wait a minute," says I to myself (my epiphany!), "what am I doing. I'm a city boy – I know nothing, absolutely nothing, about cows, or stampedes – or how to corral cows! And, my feet! Good, Lord! Have mercy on my feet!"

In the middle of my epiphany, wouldn't you know it – a big brown heifer weaved out of the herd, then bolted straight toward me. Suddenly, in a moment, the tables were turned. The "chaser" became the "chasee" – know what I mean?

I might be a city boy, but, well, the Bible promises that God will "give a way of escape" (or something like that!) and just ahead was my way of escape – an old country fence. Quick as a lick I hopped that ole wooden fence! Wouldn't you know it – that spooked heifer crashed through that fence!

Don't know how it happened but I was literally up a tree when they finally corralled the cows and that heifer.

"You can come down now, preacher!"

Hip. Hip. Hallelujah!

Prologue
So Unnecessary

A memory, like a footpath, meanders backward as I remember and recall an earlier time. I was visiting someone who lived on a farm. Behind the house was an open field and woods. At a fork in the trail that ran behind the farm house was a big red barn and a barnyard – and horses, cows, goats, pigs, and chickens.

If I sit still long enough I can still hear the sounds, see the sights and smell the pungent smells. The ground was like mush, covered with barnyard animal tracks. What I remember most, however, was the sudden flush of dark storm clouds and the rush of activity by barnyard animals as they scurried to escape the sudden downpour.

As the rain fell, harder and harder, the

farmer and I, like barnyard animals, ran for cover. Finding shelter near a chicken house we paused and what I saw next was, well, unforgettable.

As the rain continued to fall, in the middle of the barnyard a mother hen was cackling, louder and louder, calling her little chicks to shelter under her extended wings. The little chicks were racing and running for cover under the extended wings of the mother hen, escaping the rain, and the winds that swirled around them.

One little chick, however, did not heed the momma hen's call. It just stood there – alone, cold, shivering in the cold rain.

In the Bible and in life, Jesus likens himself to a mother hen, with wide, safe wings outstretched for protection and shelter in the time of storm or trouble.

In Luke's Gospel Jesus said, "how often I have longed to gather you as a hen gathers her chicks under her wings -- but you were not willing."

Hey! Is that you out there, troubled and blown about by the rough winds of life? Shivering? Alone? Sooooo Not Necessary!

Hip. Hip. Hallelujah!

John Dee Jeffries

Hip Hip Hallelujah - Book 3

JOHN DEE JEFFRIES

PUBLISHED by PARABLES
Earthly Stories with a Heavenly Meaning

www.ingramcontent.com/pod-product-compliance
Lightning Source LLC
Chambersburg PA
CBHW071752080526
44588CB00013B/2222